LITTLE CATS

Published by Creative Education, Inc., 123 South Broad Street, Mankato, Minnesota 56001

Printed by permission of Wildlife Education, Ltd.

Library of Congress Cataloging-in-Publication Data

Wexo, John Bonnett.
Little cats / by John Bonnett Wexo.
p. cm. — (Zoobooks)
Summary: Describes some of the smaller members of the cat family, including the cheetah, puma, and fishing cat.
ISBN 0-88682-413-3
1. Felidae—Juvenile literature. [1. Felidae. 2. Cats.] I. Title. II. Series: Zoo books (Mankato, Minn.)
QL737.C23W488 1991 599.74'428—dc20 91-2854 CIP AC

LITTLE CATS

Created and Written by
John Bonnett Wexo

Zoological Consultant
Charles R. Schroeder, D.V.M.
Director Emeritus
San Diego Zoo &
San Diego Wild Animal Park

Scientific Consultants
Dennis A. Meritt, Jr., Ph.D.
Assistant Director
Lincoln Park Zoo

Edward C. Schmitt
General Curator
Denver Zoo

Creative Education

Photographic Credits

Cover: Bruce Coleman, Inc.; **Pages Six and Seven:** M.J. Griffith (Photo Researchers); **Page Ten:** Lynn Rogers; **Page Twelve:** Hans Reinhard (Bruce Coleman, Ltd.); **Pages Fourteen and Fifteen:** Breck P. Kent (Animals Animals); **Page Sixteen:** Tom McHugh (Photo Researchers); **Page Seventeen:** Stephen Krasemann (DRK); **Pages Eighteen and Nineteen:** David C. Fritts (Animals Animals); **Page Twenty-one: Left,** Pat Davison (DRK); **Left Center,** Jane Howard (Photo Researchers); **Right Center,** Stephen Krasemann (DRK); **Right,** Margot Conte (Animals Animals); **Page Twenty-two:** Linda Dufurrena (Grant Heilman); **Inside Back Cover:** Marty Stouffer (Animals Animals).

Art Credits

Pages Eight and Nine: Richard Orr; **Pages Ten and Eleven:** Richard Orr; **Pages Twelve and Thirteen:** Richard Orr; **Page Twelve: Top Right,** Walter Stuart; **Page Thirteen: Top Left,** Walter Stuart; **Pages Sixteen and Seventeen:** Richard Orr; **Top,** Walter Stuart; **Page Seventeen: Middle Right,** Walter Stuart; **Pages Twenty and Twenty-one:** Richard Orr; **Page Twenty: Top Right,** Walter Stuart; **Page Twenty-one: Top Right,** Walter Stuart.

Our Thanks To: Lida Burney; Dr. Oliver Ryder (San Diego Zoo); San Diego Zoo Library Staff; Dr. Bill Newman and Dr. Fleminger (Scripps Institute of Oceanography); and Lynnette Wexo.

Contents

Little cats are among the world's most beautiful animals. All of them have wonderful glossy fur, and most of them are decorated with elegant patterns of spots and stripes. Like the Serval (SERVE-UL) shown on these pages, all little cats look mysterious and powerful. It is really easy to see why people have always found them fascinating, and why ancient people sometimes worshipped them.

Most little cats are solitary animals. They live alone and hunt alone. This is probably because it is easier for a single cat to find enough food. Once a year, male and female cats come together to mate, but they don't stay together for long.

Male and female cats of each species look a lot like each other. But the male is usually a little larger, with a bigger head. In the wild, some kinds of cats may live as long as 15 years, but most live less than 10 years.

There are many different kinds of little cats, and they live in many different kinds of places. They are found on every continent in the world except Australia and Antarctica. And they live in almost every kind of climate. Some of them live where it is hot, and some live where it is cold. Some are found where it is very dry and some where it is very wet. In fact, little cats are one of the most successful groups of animals on earth. They are found in more places than any other group of mammals.

PALLAS'S CAT
Felis manul
SNOW LEOPARD
Uncia uncia
CHINESE DESERT CAT
Felis bieti
IRIOMOTE CAT
Felis iriomotensis
ASIATIC STEPPE WILDCAT
Felis libyca ornata
LEOPARD CAT
Prionailurus bengalensis
TEMMINCK'S CAT
Profelis temmincki
FISHING CAT
Prionailurus viverrinus
JUNGLE CAT (OR REED CAT)
Felis chaus
RUSTY-SPOTTED CAT
Prionailurus rubiginosus
GOLDEN CAT
Profelis aurata
CLOUDED LEOPARD
Neofelis nebulosa
BLACK-FOOTED CAT
Felis nigripes
BORNEAN RED CAT
Pardofelis badia
FLAT-HEADED CAT
Felis planiceps
MARBLED CAT
Pardofelis marmorata

What is a "little" cat?

Strange as it may seem, scientists have had a hard time answering this question. You might think that a "little" cat is simply a cat that is little. But it is not that simple. Some little cats are very large. And a few of them are larger than some "big" cats, as you will see below.

You might think that big cats would do things in a bigger way than little cats. But this isn't always true, either. Some little cats can jump longer distances than big cats. And one little cat (the Cheetah) can run faster than any big cat. In general, little cats are also as good at hunting as big cats.

In the end, scientists have found only one thing that is always different between "big" cats and "little" cats. All big cats can roar, and all little cats cannot roar. For this reason, we might be better off if we separated the two groups of cats by the sounds they make. We could call big cats "roaring" cats and little cats "non-roaring" cats.

Like big cats, most little cats have lo tails with dark tips. But some little cats ha shorter tails, and the tails of bobcats a really short. Nobody really knows why son tails are shorter.

The Puma is the largest little cat, and the Rusty-spotted cat is the smallest. A puma can be 9 feet long (274 centimeters) including the tail. But a rusty-spotted cat may be only 2 feet long (63 centimeters) when it is fully grown. And it may weigh only 3 pounds (1.4 kilograms). Rusty-spotted cats are incredibly small. If you put four of them together, they would weigh only as much as one average house cat.

The leopard is called a "big" cat. But some "little" cats are bigger than leopards. The largest known leopard weighed 233 pounds (106 kilograms). But the largest known snow leopard weighed 286 pounds (130 kilograms). And the largest puma ever weighed was more than 300 pounds (136 kilograms).

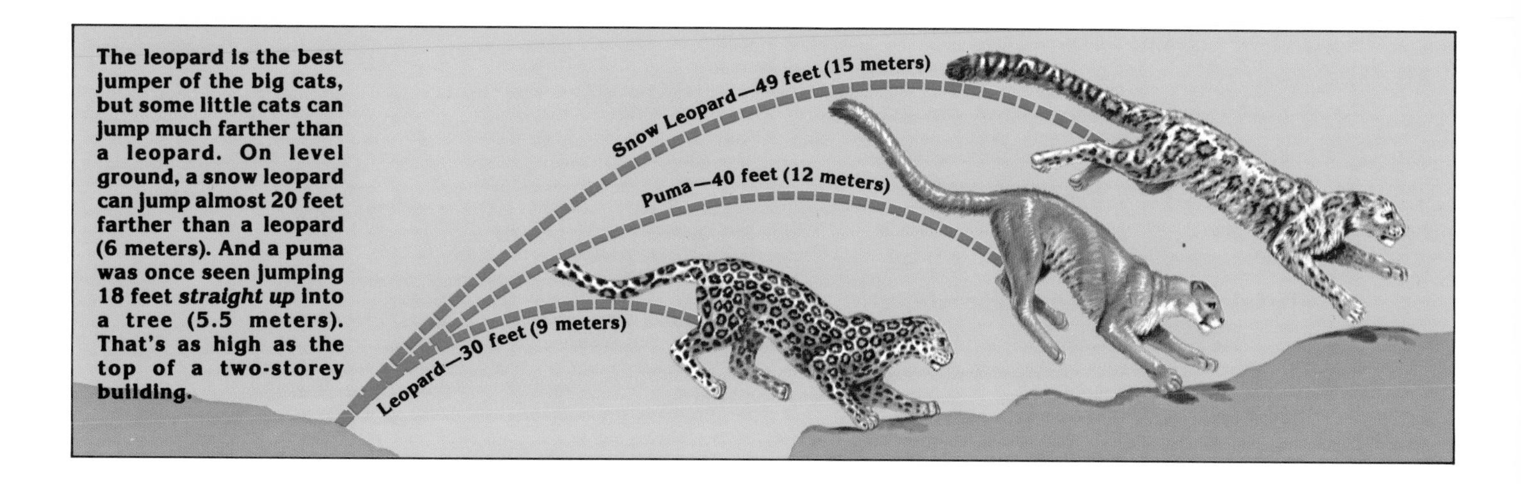

The leopard is the best jumper of the big cats, but some little cats can jump much farther than a leopard. On level ground, a snow leopard can jump almost 20 feet farther than a leopard (6 meters). And a puma was once seen jumping 18 feet *straight up* into a tree (5.5 meters). That's as high as the top of a two-storey building.

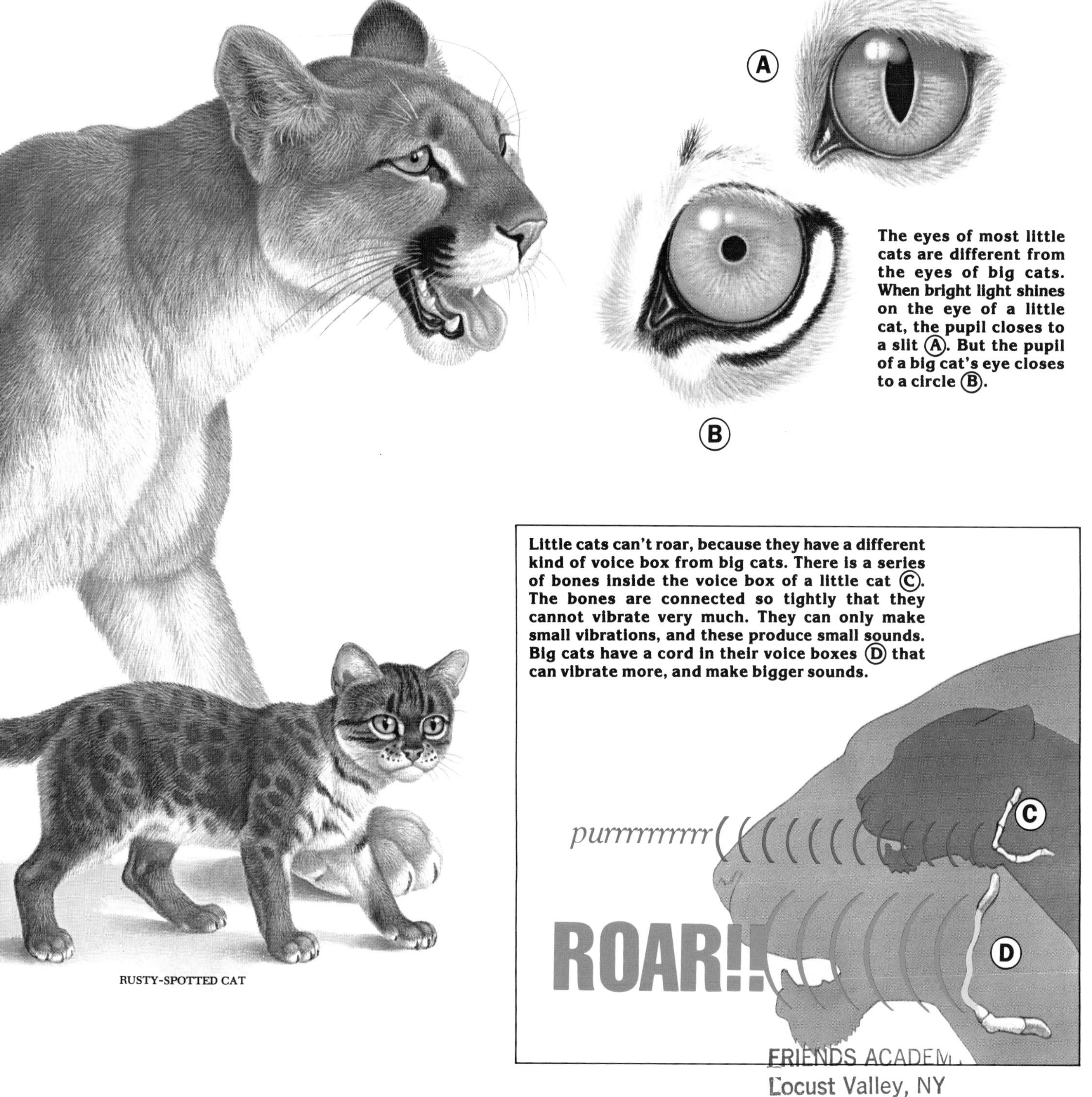

The eyes of most little cats are different from the eyes of big cats. When bright light shines on the eye of a little cat, the pupil closes to a slit (A). But the pupil of a big cat's eye closes to a circle (B).

Little cats can't roar, because they have a different kind of voice box from big cats. There is a series of bones inside the voice box of a little cat (C). The bones are connected so tightly that they cannot vibrate very much. They can only make small vibrations, and these produce small sounds. Big cats have a cord in their voice boxes (D) that can vibrate more, and make bigger sounds.

RUSTY-SPOTTED CAT

Cats are wonderful hunters.

Almost every part of a cat's body has something to do with finding prey, catching it, or eating it. For example, some cats are covered with spots or stripes, because this makes it harder to see them when they hide in trees or bushes. Other cats have plain coats that make them hard to see when they hide in grass. In both cases, the coat helps the cats get very close to their prey before they attack, as shown on the opposite page.

All little cats are meat-eaters. But different species eat different kinds of meat. Some cats eat things as small as a mouse, while a few catch prey as big as a zebra. Others eat birds, lizards, frogs, fish, and even large insects. In many places, little cats are helpful to people, because they kill rodents and other animals that destroy human crops.

Most little cats hunt at night, and they have special equipment to help them find prey in the dark. A few little cats, like the Cheetah, hunt during the day.

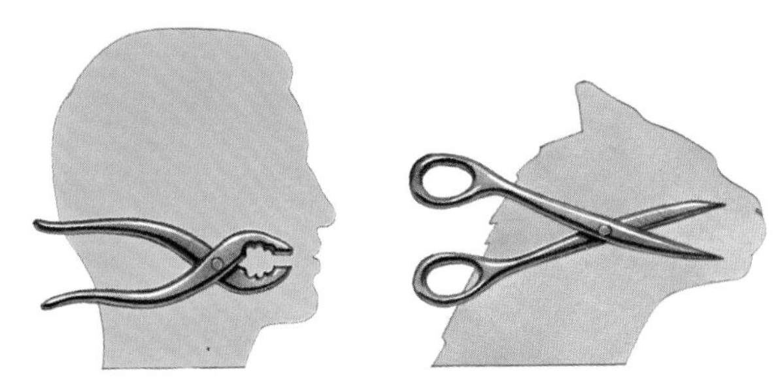

To cut meat, cats have special teeth that are very different from your teeth. Humans have cheek teeth that are flat and wide like pliers. These are used for grinding food. The cheek teeth of cats are narrow and sharp like scissors.

To hunt at night, cats need eyes that can see in the dark. Like owls, they have big eyes that are very sensitive to light. Most cats can actually see *6 times better* than people can in the dark. They are particularly good at seeing animals that are moving around. If an animal stays very still, a cat may not see it.

Cats also need good hearing to help them catch prey. In a dense forest or in thick grass, they may hear prey coming long before they can see it. Unlike humans, cats don't have to move their heads to know what direction a sound is coming from. They just move their ears.

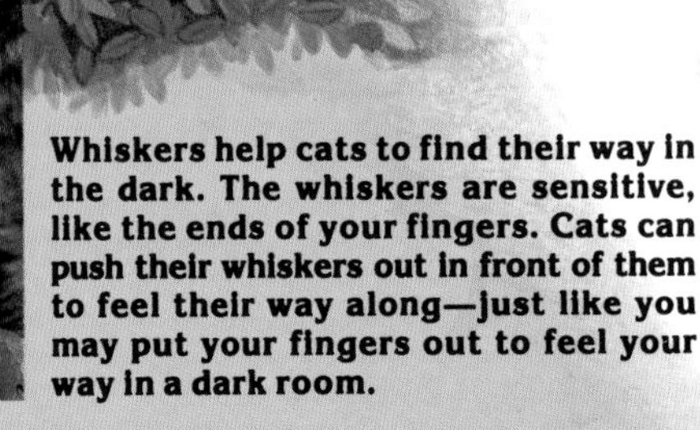

EUROPEAN WILDCAT

Whiskers help cats to find their way in the dark. The whiskers are sensitive, like the ends of your fingers. Cats can push their whiskers out in front of them to feel their way along—just like you may put your fingers out to feel your way in a dark room.

Most wild cats and house cats catch their food in the same way. They sneak up on their prey, trying to get as close as they can without being seen. This is called stalking (STAW-king). The closer the cat gets to its prey, the slower it moves. It stays close to the ground. And it hides behind bushes and rocks, to keep the prey from seeing it Ⓐ.

When the cat gets very close to its prey, it doesn't attack right away. Instead, it flattens itself against the ground and watches the prey for a while Ⓑ.

After watching the prey for some time, the cat suddenly rushes forward. It tries to knock the prey over with its paws Ⓒ.

Even though cats are very good hunters, they don't always catch the animals they go after. In fact, most cats have to stalk 10 to 20 animals before they actually catch one. Of all animals, birds are the hardest to catch. They usually fly away before the cat even gets near them.

PUMA (COUGAR)

Size can help an animal conserve body heat. A large, round body stays warm much longer than a small one. That is why a puma in Alaska is much larger than a puma found in an Amazon jungle. This animal is from southern Canada.

Cats can move with a grace and agility that is wonderful to watch. All little cats have very flexible bodies and an excellent sense of balance. And for these reasons, they can move in ways that seem next to impossible.

Most cats can walk so silently that nobody can hear them coming. Some can climb trees in the twinkling of an eye. And others can leap through the air so lightly that they almost seem to be flying.

All of this marvelous movement helps cats to hunt, of course. It helps them to get close to prey before the prey sees them. It helps them to chase prey up a tree if necessary. And it allows them to surprise prey on the ground by leaping down from a tree.

The fastest land animal on earth is a little cat—the Cheetah. Unlike other cats, the Cheetah does not stalk its prey. Instead, it chases after the prey and runs it down. From a standing start, a cheetah can reach a speed of 60 miles per hour (96 kilometers per hour) in just a few seconds. Most racing cars can't do that!

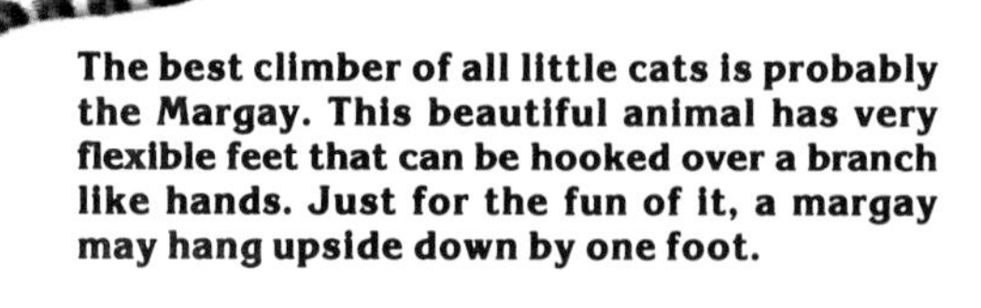

The best climber of all little cats is probably the Margay. This beautiful animal has very flexible feet that can be hooked over a branch like hands. Just for the fun of it, a margay may hang upside down by one foot.

Most cats have soft pads on the bottom of their feet to help them walk quietly. And some cats have feet that are special in other ways as well. Sand cats live in the desert, and they have thick mats of hair on the bottom of their feet. The mats protect the feet from the hot sand. The Lynx (LINK-s) lives in the north and has to walk on snow. It has broad feet that spread the weight of the cat like snowshoes. The wide feet keep the lynx from sinking too deeply into the snow, as shown below.

All little cats will climb trees to escape danger, but only a few species are really good climbers. Clouded leopards are among the best climbers. They do most of their hunting in trees, and can run up and down tree trunks like squirrels.

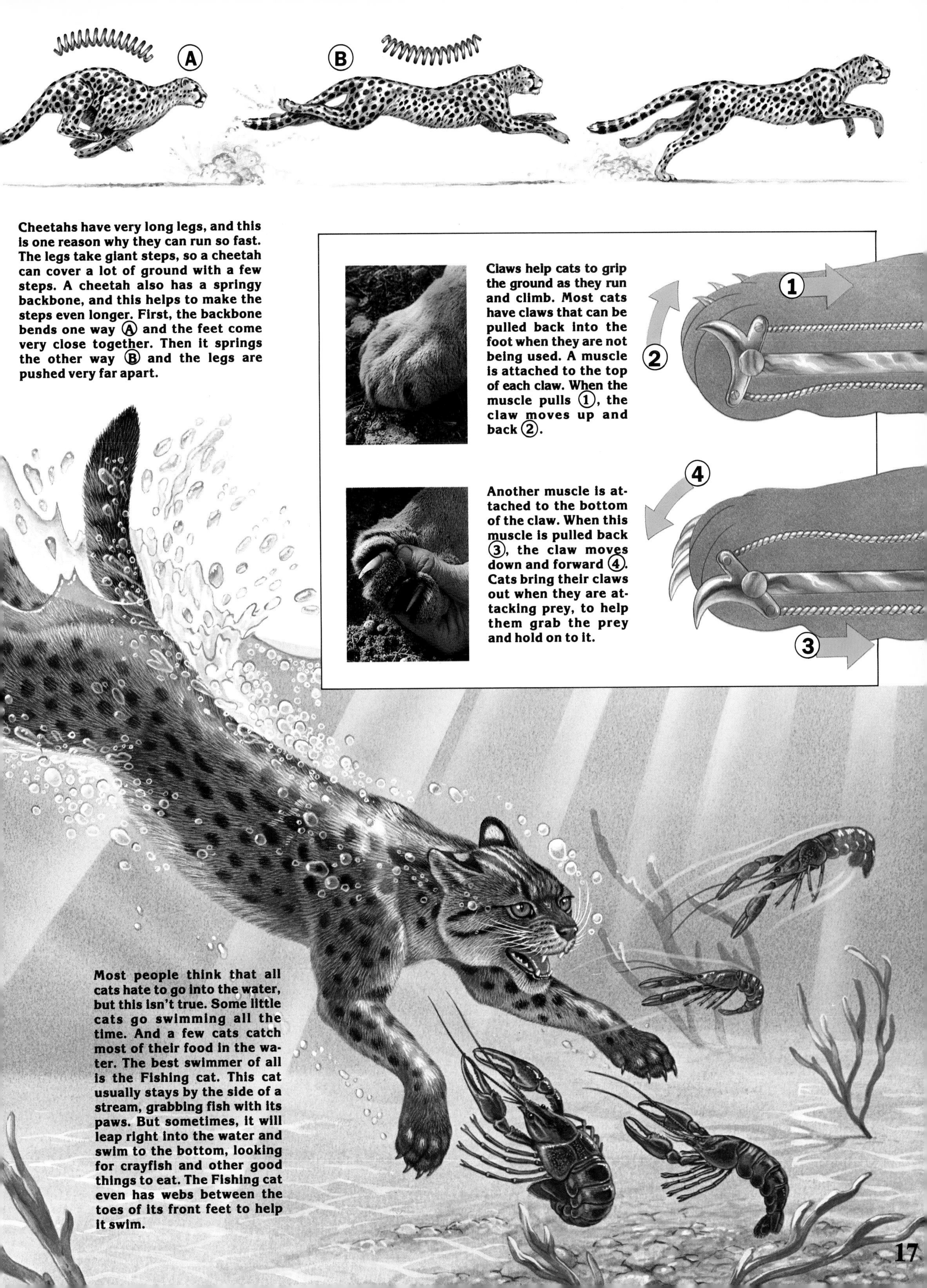

Cheetahs have very long legs, and this is one reason why they can run so fast. The legs take giant steps, so a cheetah can cover a lot of ground with a few steps. A cheetah also has a springy backbone, and this helps to make the steps even longer. First, the backbone bends one way Ⓐ and the feet come very close together. Then it springs the other way Ⓑ and the legs are pushed very far apart.

Claws help cats to grip the ground as they run and climb. Most cats have claws that can be pulled back into the foot when they are not being used. A muscle is attached to the top of each claw. When the muscle pulls ①, the claw moves up and back ②.

Another muscle is attached to the bottom of the claw. When this muscle is pulled back ③, the claw moves down and forward ④. Cats bring their claws out when they are attacking prey, to help them grab the prey and hold on to it.

Most people think that all cats hate to go into the water, but this isn't true. Some little cats go swimming all the time. And a few cats catch most of their food in the water. The best swimmer of all is the Fishing cat. This cat usually stays by the side of a stream, grabbing fish with its paws. But sometimes, it will leap right into the water and swim to the bottom, looking for crayfish and other good things to eat. The Fishing cat even has webs between the toes of its front feet to help it swim.

Cheetahs require great bursts of energy to attain speeds of 60 m.p.h. or more, and so must rest between hunts. Here a mother cheetah tries to doze while her four cubs stay awake and curious.

The ancestor of all house cats was probably the African wildcat. Most wild cats cannot be trained to live with people as domestic animals. But African wildcats can be very friendly to people and were probably easy to train.

Most scientists believe that African wildcats were first turned into domestic cats in Egypt, about 4,000 years ago. Since that time, people have taken domestic cats with them to many parts of the world, and cat lovers have developed many breeds of cats. Today, there are more than 500 million domestic cats in the world, with 33 different breeds.

The various breeds look very different from each other, with many different hair patterns and colors. But under the skin, they all look very much like African wildcats. And no matter how tame they may seem, they still behave like wild cats at times.

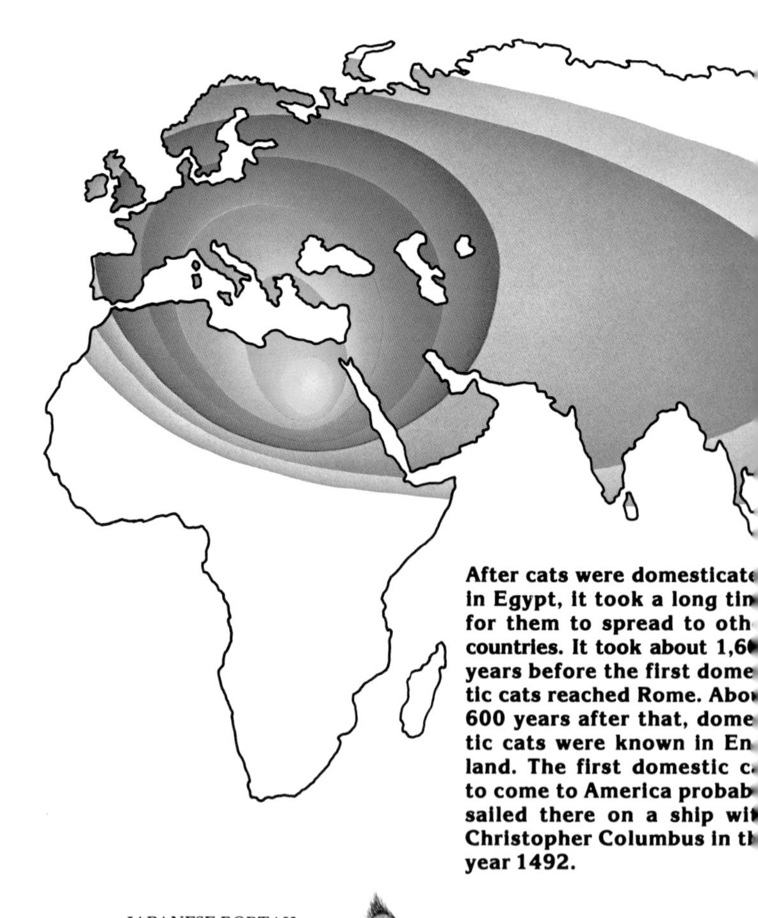

After cats were domesticat in Egypt, it took a long tin for them to spread to oth countries. It took about 1,6 years before the first dome tic cats reached Rome. Abo 600 years after that, dome tic cats were known in En land. The first domestic c to come to America probab sailed there on a ship wi Christopher Columbus in t year 1492.

Egyptians worshipped cats as gods. It was a crime to hurt a cat, and anybody who did was put to death. It was also a crime to take cats out of Egypt. And this is probably why it took so long for domestic cats to spread to other countries. The cats had to be smuggled out of the country, as shown at right. Can you find the cat in the picture?

Many things that are done by domestic cats show that they still have a lot of wild cat in them. For instance, domestic cat mothers carry their babies around in the same way that wild cat mothers do.

Wild cats sometimes mark their territories by scratching on trees. This is to warn other cats to stay away. At other times, wild cats may scratch on trees to sharpen their claws. Domestic cats scratch furniture for the same reasons. From the cat's point of view, the house it lives in is its territory. And the people who think they own the cat are really just guests in the cat's territory.

The future of little cats is uncertain. Like many other kinds of wild animals, cats are in trouble today because people are doing things that are harmful to them. If people will change some of their ways, the little cats will survive on this earth. But if people refuse to change, the cats will not survive.

People hurt cats in three major ways. First, there are people who are killing some of the most beautiful cats to get their spotted and striped skins. Most people feel that these skins are more beautiful when they are left on a living animal. But a few selfish people are not happy unless they can have coats made of the skins. They don't care how many cats must be destroyed to help them show off in this way.

People also kill wild cats to keep them from preying on farm animals, such as chickens and other small livestock. These people don't realize that cats often make up for the livestock they eat by killing many animals that destroy human crops. The value of crops that cats save is far greater than the value of the livestock they take.

Finally, people harm little cats by destroying their habitat—the land they need to live on. The land is taken from the animals to build farms, factories, and houses on it. And in many places, there is no room left for wild cats.

If we want to have little cats in this world, we must stop people from making coats out of their skins. We must start appreciating the help that cats give to ranchers and farmers. And we must make sure that there will always be enough wild places in which they can live.

Where does a little cat belong? Is it in a trap, like the Bobcat above? Is it on somebody's back as a fur coat? Or is it in the wild, running free?

Index